Copyright © 2024 Hilda R

All rights reserved

No part of this book may be reproduced, or stored in a retrieval system, or transmitted in any form or by any means, electronic, mechanical, photocopying, recording, or otherwise, without express written permission of the publisher.

Dedication

Thank you to my wonderful husband Dave, and to my amazing "kids" Tim and Danielle. You've been hearing about me writing a book for a long time and it's finally here. I couldn't have done it without you cheering me on! Thanks for all the ways you love and support our family Dave, so that I can do what I love to do. And thank you for always believing in me. The three of you are my world. I love you.

DECLUTTERING
From A to Z

HILDA RODGERS

CONTENTS

Acknowledgements

My Journey From Overwhelmed to Organized

Introductions

1. Why Declutter?
2. Getting Ready to Donate
3. Trash and Recycling
4. Decluttering "A" Things
5. Decluttering "B" Things
6. Decluttering "C" Things
7. Decluttering "D" Things
8. Decluttering "E" Things
9. Decluttering "F" Things
10. Decluttering "G" Things
11. Decluttering "H" Things
12. Decluttering "I" Things
13. Decluttering "J" Things
14. Decluttering "K" Things
15. Decluttering "L" Things
16. Decluttering "M" Things
17. Decluttering "N" Things
18. Decluttering "O" Things
19. Decluttering "P" Things
20. Decluttering "Q" Things
21. Decluttering "R" Things
22. Decluttering "S" Things
23. Decluttering "T" Things
24. Decluttering "U" Things

25. Decluttering "V" Things

26. Decluttering "W" Things

27. Decluttering "X" Things

28. Decluttering "Y" Things

29. Decluttering "Z" Things

30. What Now?

Resources

Bonus

About the Author

ACKNOWLEDGMENTS

Books don't come together overnight or by themselves, and I'd like to acknowledge those who helped bring this book to life.

Thank you, Adele Lapointe and Pamela Wong. Your encouragement and accountability on our working getaways laid the foundation for this book and your ongoing support throughout the writing process was invaluable! Adele, you inspired me to write a book after I watched you write yours, and your experience and guidance made things easier for me. Pam, your attention to detail in all aspects of this book helped me fine tune things just the way my organized brain wanted them but that I couldn't always see clearly along the way.

Thank you to the members of the 365 Items in 365 Days Facebook group, who contributed many of the letter ideas when I first launched the Decluttering From A To Z challenge several years ago. I wasn't sure how the idea would go over, but you jumped in, had fun, decluttered a lot, and were creative with the items that started with different letters. Especially the challenging ones!

Thank you, Maria Santiago, for your design help on the front and back cover and for making all my different purples match!

Thank you Sheila Penton and Amanda Gavigan for all your help formatting this book and helping me prepare to launch it.

Thank you to my amazing team organizers at From Overwhelmed to Organized for all the extra organizing you've done for my clients while I've been working on this book. Cheryl Stirling, Rick Baiilargeon, Diane Woodworth, and the previously mentioned Adele Lapointe and Pamela Wong, you are incredible organizers, colleagues, and friends.

And last but certainly not least, thank you to my parents, Dirk and Triny Potma for teaching me the alphabet. That song was in my head over and over throughout the writing of this book! Thank you for raising me to believe I can do anything I put my mind to and getting me started on my organizing journey at a young age.

My Journey From
OVERWHELMED TO ORGANIZED

I have always loved organizing. I enjoy finding solutions to challenges and improving the way things work. But sometimes life gets in the way of being as organized as we'd like to be, and it doesn't take much to become overwhelmed in our own homes. I know, because I've been there.

After a busy career in adult education, while raising two young children, my home had become cluttered and disorganized. I was overwhelmed! But I made time to declutter and organize my home and it changed everything.

I shared my journey on my blog and I came to see that many people are overwhelmed with the clutter and lack of organization in their homes. I started giving decluttering and organizing tips on my blog to help people take back control of their homes.

I realized that in addition to helping people online, I wanted to help people organize their homes in person, so I became a professional organizer. Now I have the pleasure of helping clients both hands on and virtually, and I love seeing the difference a bit of decluttering and organizing makes in their lives. My education background also gives me skills to teach my clients how to maintain the systems we set up.

If you're reading this book, you probably feel at least somewhat overwhelmed. I understand how you feel right now, and I do not pass judgement on you or the state of your home.

Our homes should be peaceful and calm. They should be places where we can relax, and spend time doing the things we enjoy doing, with the people we love. If you want that for your home, then please keep reading.

I hope this book helps you on your journey from overwhelmed to organized! - Hilda

INTRODUCTION

Whether you need to do a lot of decluttering or just a little, this book will be perfect for you. The first few chapters contain some general decluttering tips. The rest of the chapters are based on the letters of the alphabet and each have: a decluttering tip, a list of ideas of things you can declutter, and an inspirational quote, that are all featuring that letter. You can declutter anything you want from the list, or come up with your own ideas!

There are lots of wonderful books available that help you declutter room by room, but that system doesn't work for everyone.

First of all, it can be overwhelming to think about decluttering a whole room, especially if you have a lot of clutter. But decluttering by letter gives you control over what you let go of so you don't feel as overwhelmed.

Secondly, if you've already decluttered a room, but you still feel like you can let go of more, it's helpful to look at your belongings in a different way. Decluttering by letter gives you a different lens through which to see what you own.

And lastly, you may not store all of a particular item in the same room. If you only ever declutter by room, you may not realize how many of a particular item you have until you declutter by letter and gather everything in one category in one place.

So whether you're new to decluttering, have attempted to declutter but got discouraged, or have been decluttering for years and need a fresh approach to get you motivated again, decluttering by letter can help you!

Wherever you are in your decluttering journey, Decluttering From A To Z is for you!

How To Use "Decluttering From A To Z"

Are you ready to declutter from A to Z? Want some decluttering ideas, tips, and inspiration? Here are some ways to get the most out of this book.

Decluttering from A to Z is completely flexible.
- I'm not telling you how much you have to declutter... that's totally up to you!
- I'm also not telling you what you have to declutter... that's also up to you!
- I'm not telling you when you have to declutter... again, how often and how long are completely up to you!

This book is simply here to give you ideas and inspiration to help you to declutter.

As you go through the book, pick one item that resonates with you and go declutter those things! If you're on a roll, you can pick another item. The next day or next week (or whatever schedule you create), you can move onto a new letter, or pick another item from the same letter. Whatever helps you let go of things!

The beauty of this is that you have total control over what you declutter and you can keep coming back to this book for ideas when you're feeling stuck. There are hundreds of different categories! It may help you declutter items in your home that you may not have thought about decluttering before.

The idea of decluttering from A to Z started as a challenge in my 365 Items in 365 Days Facebook group and it was a lot of fun. Yes, decluttering can be fun! We decluttered every day for one month, focusing on a different letter each day. Everyone shared the items they were decluttering that started with that letter. We got pretty creative with some letters!

Ready to Declutter?

I hope the ideas in this book will help you on your decluttering journey! You can inspire others, and hold yourself accountable, by sharing your pictures in any of these places:

- The 365 Items in 365 Days Facebook group (ask to join if you're not already a member)
- On social media using the hashtag #DeclutteringFromAToZ

1. Why Declutter?

Before we start decluttering, I want you to think about why you want to declutter. Reflecting on your motivation will help you make decisions on what you can let go of and what you want to keep.

Why Declutter?

Everyone's motivations for decluttering are different. Here are some ways that clutter may be affecting your life:

- You are embarrassed to have friends or family over because of the clutter in your home
- You are often frustrated because you can't find things when you need them
- You frequently pay bills late because they get buried in a pile of papers on your kitchen counter
- You can't eat at your dining room table because it's filled with stuff
- Your kids have plenty of toys but rarely play with them because there are too many of them all over the playroom floor
- You often run late in the morning because you can't find a thing to wear in your overstuffed closet
- You can't relax in your living room because there are piles of clutter on every surface
- You're not productive in your home office because there is paperwork and clutter piled up on the desk, shelves, and floor.
- You get overwhelmed when you walk in the door and see all the clutter everywhere

Do any of these sound familiar? **Please know that you are not alone!** I've felt most of these things at one point in time (even as I write this, I need to declutter my office!). I've helped lots of people declutter, both online and in person, and one of the things they are often relieved to find out is that most people, including myself, struggle with clutter to varying degrees.

Ask yourself these questions:
- What do you want your home to look like?
- How do you want to feel when you're at home?
- What is your vision for your home?

Write down your reason(s) for decluttering here:

_____

The First Step - Your Goals & Vision

Now that you've thought about why you want to declutter, set a goal of what you want to accomplish. Consider what action(s) you can take towards achieving that goal.

Here are some examples:

- If your goal is to declutter your entry area and living room so you can have guests over, then send out invitations for a date next month. Nothing motivates me to declutter as much as having people over!
- If you want to declutter your playroom so your kids can enjoy their toys more, then book a playdate for a month from now. You can even get your kids involved in decluttering and use the playdate to keep them motivated.
- If your goal is to be able to get ready quickly in the morning, schedule a charity pick-up for a few weeks from now to pick up all the clothing you're going to purge by then. It will be easier to let go of things when you know they're going to a good cause and having that deadline will keep you from procrastinating if you get stuck.

These are just examples, but you get the idea. Goals are much more likely to be achieved if you have a realistic deadline!

Write down your goals and the steps you need to take to help you reach them:

_____
_____
_____
_____
_____

Refer to these goals throughout the book. Your choices of what you keep and what you declutter should be based on your vision for your home. Keep things that will help you achieve your vision. Let go of things that don't.

A word of caution... don't set a goal that is too lofty. Most likely your clutter didn't accumulate overnight and it won't go away that quickly either.

Share Your Vision and Goals!

As you prepare to declutter, tell a friend or family member, or share on your social media channels what your motivation and your goals are. This will help keep you accountable and increase the likelihood of achieving your goals. You might inspire them to start decluttering themselves and you can cheer each other on.

A great way to stay motivated when decluttering is to take pictures of what you've decluttered, or take before and after pictures. These pictures can be motivating if you get discouraged along the way. You can look back on what you've already done and see the progress. That can help you get back on track so you can achieve your goals.

Please don't feel embarrassed by your before pictures... we're all in this together! You don't have to share your pictures with anyone but take them for yourself at least. If you do want to share them in a safe place for accountability, join the 365 Items in 365 Days Facebook group. Only group members (fellow declutterers) will see your photos. We'll all cheer you on! It's a very supportive group.

DECLUTTERING FROM A TO Z

2. Getting Ready to Donate

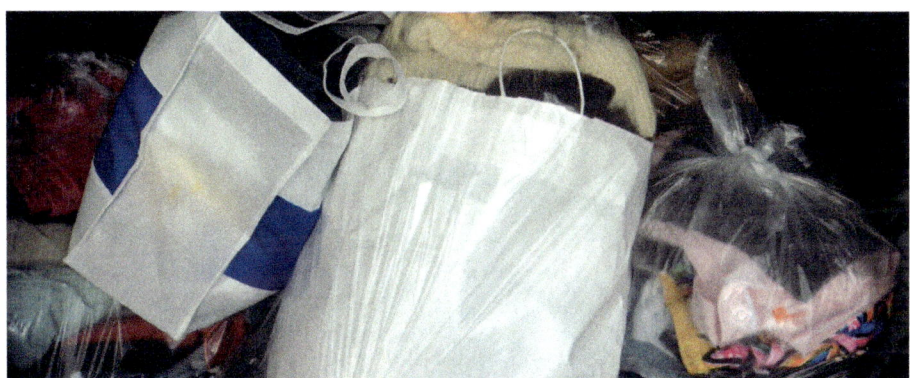
Image: Bags in the trunk

In this chapter we're talking about donations: why it's good to donate, what kinds of things you can donate, where you can donate, and how to make it easy to donate, as you declutter.

Why Should I Donate?

As you declutter, you'll come across things you're ready to let go of, but that are in good enough condition that other people can still use them. If you have friends or family members who you can give things to, that's a great option. It's fun seeing someone else use something that used to be yours. Young adults moving away from home or newlyweds just starting out could benefit from your excess furniture, linens, and household items. Families with younger children might appreciate hand-me-down clothes and toys.

You can also donate those items to local charities, especially if you have a charity that's special to you. Most charities will pass them on or sell the items and put the money towards people in need. It feels good knowing your possessions can support their cause.

It also helps you let go when you know your belongings can really benefit someone else. Instead of something taking up space in your home, give it to someone who will actually use it and appreciate it.

Donating also helps keep items out of landfills, which is good for the environment.

Write down your reason(s) for donating items here:
_____
_____

11

What Can I Donate?

So what kinds of things can you donate? Here are some commonly donated items:
- Clothing
- Books
- Toys
- Household items
- Small appliances
- Electronics
- Furniture
- Linens
- Stuffed animals

Just make sure items are clean and in good working condition. Think about the people who will benefit from your things and what they would want given to them. Most charities are run by volunteers and they don't have the resources to fix broken items or get rid of unusable things.

Where Can I Donate?

The list of places you can give away your belongings is unlimited! Here are a few ideas to get you started:
- Shelters (abused women, young moms, etc.)
- Community centers
- Church-run community programs
- Youth programs
- Big Brothers / Big Sisters programs
- Fire Halls (they give like-new stuffed animals to kids after a fire)
- Animal shelters (they love linens!)
- Habitat for Humanity Re-Stores
- Church rummage sales
- Salvation Army
- Thrift stores
- Online groups helping people in need (newcomers, homeless, etc.)
- Local buy nothing or Freecycle groups

Do some research into charities and organizations in your area to find out what their needs are, as well as what they don't accept.

Write down some charities in your area as well as what they accept and don't accept:

DECLUTTERING FROM A TO Z

_____
_____
_____
_____
_____

How To Make Donating Easy For Yourself

Some people throw most of their belongings away once they start decluttering because they feel it's too much work to donate things. But it doesn't have to be hard.

Here are a few ways to make it easy to donate:

- Set up a donation box in a conspicuous place in your home and any time you come across something you want to donate, add it to the box. Teach everyone in your family to do the same. When it's full, drop it off wherever you're donating it. I created some printable decluttering signs that you can download and print if that will help you (see the Resources page)!
- While you're in the midst of decluttering, it's good to have several large bags or empty boxes handy so you can easily add any donate-able items to them as you work. I usually use clear garbage bags so your donated items aren't accidentally confused with garbage and thrown away. Keep some tape and a marker handy to label bags or boxes too.
- Make donating part of your weekly routine. Find a time in your weekly schedule when you're driving near a donation center and make a point of dropping off donations every week at that time. You're nearby anyway so it's easy to pull up and drop off a bag or box.
- Many charities will pick up donations from your porch or driveway. Check what's available in your area. It's an easy way to get items from your home into the right hands! Here's a picture of donations on my porch (they're marked with a D for Diabetes as instructed).

Image: Donations on the driveway

13

Write down a few things you can do to make it easier to donate your decluttered items:
_____
_____
_____

Which charities in your area will pick up donations and how do you schedule a pick-up?
_____
_____
_____

3. Trash and Recycling

Image: Bins for sorting

Let's discuss garbage and recycling. A lot of clutter in our homes is actually garbage or recycling. It's not stuff we'll use again and it's not in good enough condition to donate or give away. Before you start decluttering, let's talk about how to deal with the garbage and recycling clutter you'll come across.

As you're decluttering, you'll want to donate or give away (or even sell if possible) as many items as you can to avoid sending usable items to the landfill. But for everything that isn't usable, toss it in the garbage or recycling.

With the amount of garbage and recycling you'll hopefully be tossing as you declutter, spend a bit extra and get good quality bags. You'll save time and money!

- I recommend using black garbage bags for garbage and blue bags for recycling (or whatever is standard where you live)
- Depending on what kind of trash you are eliminating, you may want to use odour shield bags so things don't get too smelly
- Contractor grade garbage bags are helpful if you have a lot of trash because they don't tear as easily
- Empty cardboard boxes work well for recycling too, especially if you're decluttering a lot of paper (it weighs more than other recycling so you can't fit as much in the blue bags)

Professional Organizer Tip:

You get what you pay for with cheap bags. They don't hold as much (so you end up using more of them which costs as much in the end as better quality bags), they rip easily (and who wants to spend time cleaning up when bags break or tear?), and if you're limited by how much garbage you can put at the curb, then larger, stronger bags are definitely better.

If your area only accepts garbage or recycling in bins, then you can still gather everything in bags in your home and empty them into the bins. This makes the decluttering process easier as you go.

Write down your local waste management's rules for what items are acceptable in the garbage and what items can be recycled

_____
_____
_____

Write down where any special kinds of waste need to go and what the hours are for those facilities (electronic waste, batteries, chemicals, etc.)

_____
_____
_____

A Note About Shredding

If you're decluttering mail or other paperwork, you'll probably come across items you should shred. Anything with addresses, account numbers, or confidential information should be shredded instead of recycled.

For small amounts, you can designate a bin or a box for shredding, and when you're finished gathering it all, you can take a few minutes and shred it yourself.

If you find you have a lot to shred all at once while you're decluttering or if you don't own a shredder, you may need to consider having it shredded somewhere else.

Write down the shredding companies in your area, along with their fees and procedures.

_____
_____
_____

Ready to Declutter From A to Z?

Now that you've thought about why you want to declutter, what your goals are, where you'll take items you're donating, and how you'll deal with garbage and recycling, you're ready to get started!

Happy decluttering!

DECLUTTERING FROM A TO Z

4. Decluttering "A" Things

Image: Appliances

ACCOUNTABILITY helps you stay on track

In this chapter you're decluttering items that begin with the letter A. You can declutter *anything you want* that begins with A. Choose any of the items below that resonate with you, or declutter your own ideas that begin with A.

Decluttering Ideas That Begin With The Letter A

Here are a few items or areas you may have in your home that you could declutter:
- Stuff you have an **Abundance** of
- **Accessories**
- **Acetaminophen**
- Equipment related to **Activities** you or your family members no longer do
- **Alcohol** (stuff you know you'll never use... this isn't a free pass to drink all day LOL!)
- **Alcove**
- **All** the things in a specific category you no longer use
- **Aloe**
- **Already** used things
- **Alumni** magazines

17

- **Ancient** comforters
- Stuffed **Animals**
- **Anti**-anything medications
- **Antibiotics**
- **Antique** things
- **Apple** products and gadgets
- **Apple**-themed decor
- **Appliances**
- **Aprons**
- **Arm** chairs
- **Armoires**
- **Artificial** anything
- **Artificial** flowers
- **Athletic** awards
- **Athletic** equipment
- **Atlases**
- **Attic**
- **Audio**-visual stuff
- **Automobile**
- Things that aren't **Awesome**
- And if none of those apply then just declutter **Anything**!

Find a few of these things that you no longer need, use, love, or have the space to store (that's the definition of clutter by the way!) and let them go.

Write here the items you decluttered that begin with A:
_____
_____
_____
_____

"AT its heart, clutter is a lack of peace." ~ Kathi Lipp

DECLUTTERING FROM A TO Z

5. Decluttering "B" Things

Image: Batteries

BEGIN with items that are easy to let go of

In this chapter you're decluttering items that begin with the letter B. You can declutter *anything you want* that begins with B. Choose any of the items below that resonate with you, or declutter your own ideas that begin with B.

Decluttering Ideas That Begin With The Letter B

Here are a few items or areas you may have in your home that you could declutter:
- **Baby** clothes
- Any other **Baby** items
- **Bags** (reusable or plastic)
- **Ball**-point pens
- **Balls**
- **Banjos**
- **BBQ** tools/equipment
- Under the **Bed**
- **Bedrooms**
- **Beer** cans/**Bottles** (once again, drinking all day doesn't count)
- **Bee**-sting medication

19

- **Belts**
- **Bibles**
- **Bike** gear
- **Bikes**
- **Bills**
- **Binoculars**
- **Birthday** cards
- **Blue** items
- **Board** games
- **Bobbleheads**
- **Books**
- **Borrowed** items
- **Bottles** of nail polish
- Any kind of **Bottles**
- **Bows**
- **Boxes** (products, decorative, moving, food, for projects)
- **Boys'** stuff
- **Bracelets**
- **Bras**
- **Broken** things
- **Brown** items
- **Brushes**
- **Bumpy** socks
- **Burnt** out candles
- **Burnt** out light bulbs
- **Buttons**

Find a few of these things that you no longer need, use, love, or have the space to store and let them go.

Write here the items you decluttered that begin with B:
_____
_____
_____
_____

> *"BE content with what you have; rejoice in the way things are. When you realize there is nothing lacking, the whole world belongs to you."* ~ Lao Tzu

6. Decluttering "C" Things

Image: Clothing

CREATE a plan to declutter regularly

In this chapter you're decluttering items that begin with the letter C. You can declutter *anything you want* that begins with C. Choose any of the items below that resonate with you, or declutter your own ideas that begin with C.

Decluttering Ideas That Begin With The Letter C

Here are a few items or areas you may have in your home that you could declutter:

- **Cabinets**
- **Camera** equipment
- **Cameras**
- **Camisoles**
- **Camping** equipment
- **Candle** holders
- **Candles**
- **Candy**
- **Canned** food
- **Caps**
- **Cards**

- Gift **Cards**
- **Cars**
- Toy **Cars**
- **Cartons**
- **Casserole** dishes
- **Cat** items
- **CD's**
- **Chairs** (either the actual chairs or the stuff piled up on them)
- **Cherry** coloured items
- **Chess/Checkers** games
- Toy **Chests**
- **Childhood** memorabilia
- **China** cabinet
- **China** sets
- **Chocolate** (but really why would you declutter that?!)
- **Chocolate** coloured items
- **Cleaning** supplies
- **Clips** (hair, paper, chip, etc.)
- **Clocks**
- **Closets**
- **Clothing**
- **Clutch** purses
- **Coasters**
- **Coats**
- **Coins**
- Any kind of **Collection**
- **College** memorabilia
- **Colour** TV's
- **Comforters**
- Items in your **Command Centre**
- **Computer** parts/accessories
- **Construction** paper
- **Contacts** list
- **Containers**
- **Cookbooks**
- **Cookies**

- **Cookie** sheets
- **Cooking** utensils
- Apple **Corers**
- **Cosmetics**
- **Couches**
- **Cough/Cold** medicine
- **Counters**
- **Coupons**
- **Craft** supplies
- **Crap** (not a term you'd typically hear a professional organizer use, but it's a good generic term!)
- **Crayons**
- Pencil **Crayons**
- **Crepe** paper (streamers)
- **Crib** sheets
- **Crisper** drawers in the fridge
- **Crochet** supplies
- **Crock** pots
- **Cross**-stitch supplies/kits
- **Cupboards**
- **Cups**
- **Curtains**
- **Cutlery**

Find a few of these things that you no longer need, use, love, or have the space to store and let them go.

Write here the items you decluttered that begin with C:
_____
_____
_____
_____

> "*CLUTTER is not just the stuff on your floor - it's anything that stands between you and the life you want to be living.*" ~ Peter Walsh

DECLUTTERING FROM A TO Z

7. Decluttering "D" Things

Image: Dishes

DONATE items you aren't using so someone else can use them

In this chapter you're decluttering items that begin with the letter D. You can declutter *anything you want* that begins with D. Choose any of the items below that resonate with you, or declutter your own ideas that begin with D.

Decluttering Ideas That Begin With The Letter D

Here are a few items or areas you may have in your home that you could declutter:
- **Daddy's** things (with his permission!)
- **Data** sticks
- **Deck** boxes
- **Deck** furniture
- **Delayed Decisions**
- **Desktops**
- **Dictionaries**
- **Digital** files
- Toy **Dinosaurs**
- **Discounted** items
- **Dishcloths**

25

- **Dishes**
- **Dog** items
- **Dolls** (and/or **Doll** clothes, **Doll** accessories, etc.)
- **Dominoes**
- Things you have **Doubles** or **Duplicates** or **Dozens** of
- **Drawers** (kitchen, dresser, etc.)
- **Drawings**
- **Dressers**
- **Dresses**
- **Driftwood** pieces
- The top of the **Dryer**
- **DVD's**

Find a few of these things that you no longer need, use, love, or have the space to store and let them go.

Write here the items you decluttered that begin with D:

_____
_____
_____
_____

"*DONE is better than perfect.*" ~ Sheryl Sandberg

8. Decluttering "E" Things

Image: Electronics

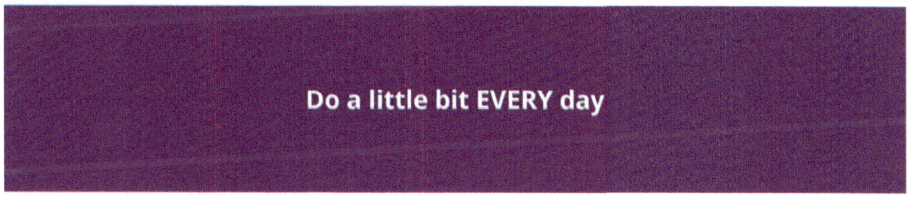

In this chapter you're decluttering items that begin with the letter E. You can declutter *anything you want* that begins with E. Choose any of the items below that resonate with you, or declutter your own ideas that begin with E.

Decluttering Ideas That Begin With The Letter E

Here are a few items or areas you may have in your home that you could declutter:

- **Earbuds**
- **Earmuffs**
- **Earrings**
- Anything else you use for your **Ears**
- **Easy** to purge items
- Things you **Eat**
- Things you use when you're **Eating**
- **Ebooks**
- **Educational** stuff
- **Egg** cartons
- Items you have **Eight** of

27

- **Elastics**
- **Electrical** bits & pieces
- **Electronics**
- **Elliptical**
- **Emails**
- **Encyclopedias**
- Book **Ends**
- Things you have more than **Enough** of
- **Envelopes**
- Any kind of **Equipment**
- **Erasers**
- **Everything**!
- Things from an **Ex**
- **Exercise** DVD's
- **Exercise Equipment**
- **Exercise** wear
- **Eye** glasses
- **Eye** liner
- **Eye** shadow
- Anything else you use for your **Eyes**

Find a few of these things that you no longer need, use, love, or have the space to store and let them go.

Write here the items you decluttered that begin with D:
_____
_____
_____
_____

> "There's a legit benefit to getting rid of stuff you don't need or want—less to clean, manage, and maintain. But perhaps my favorite reason to declutter my life is this: EVERYTHING that remains is beautiful." ~ Tsh Oxenreider

DECLUTTERING FROM A TO Z

9. Decluttering "F" Things

Image: Flip Flops

FOCUS on your progress, not about getting things perfect

In this chapter you're decluttering items that begin with the letter F. You can declutter *anything you want* that begins with F. Choose any of the items below that resonate with you, or declutter your own ideas that begin with F.

Decluttering Ideas That Begin With The Letter F

Here are a few items or areas you may have in your home that you could declutter:
- **Facebook Friends** or pages you **Follow**
- **Face** powder (or anything for your **Face**)
- **Facial** cleansers
- **Fairies**
- **Fake Fruit**
- **Fall** decor
- **Family** room
- Things you're keeping out of **Fear** (fear of hurting the person who gave it to you, fear you'll need it someday, etc.)
- **Feather** pillows
- **Feathers**

29

- Anything for your **Feet**
- **Felt**
- Old/extra **Feminine** products
- **Fiction** books
- **Fish** bowls
- **Fishing** equipment
- **Fitness** gear/equipment
- Items that need to be **Fixed** (that you'll never fix!)
- **Flamingos**
- **Flat** surfaces
- **Fleas**
- **Flip Flops**
- **Floors**
- **Fondue** sets
- **Foolish** purchases
- Things you've **Forgotten** about
- Items you have **Four** or **Five** or **Fifty** of
- **Fragrances**
- Picture **Frames**
- Your old "**Frankie** says relax" shirt :)
- Anything you got for **Free**
- **Freezer**
- **Fridge**
- Items that belong to **Friends** or **Family**
- **Frisbees**
- **Frogs**
- **Funnels**

Find a few of these things that you no longer need, use, love, or have the space to store and let them go.

Write here the items you decluttered that begin with F:
_____
_____
_____
_____

"FOR the longest time, I thought I needed to be more organized. Now I know I just needed less stuff." ~ Alysa Bajenaru

10. Decluttering "G" Things

Image: Gloves

Think about what you GAIN by decluttering, not what you lose

In this chapter you're decluttering items that begin with the letter G. You can declutter *anything you want* that begins with G. Choose any of the items below that resonate with you, or declutter your own ideas that begin with G.

Decluttering Ideas That Begin With The Letter G

Here are a few items or areas you may have in your home that you could declutter:

- **Gallon**-sized jars
- **Galoshes**
- **Games**
- **Garage**
- **Garbage**
- **Gardening** magazines
- **Gardening** tools
- **Giant** picture books
- **Gift** cards
- **Gifts** (that you were given and never use or that you were planning to give but never gave)

DECLUTTERING FROM A TO Z

- **Gift** wrap
- **Girl** stuff
- **Glass**
- Things made of **Glass**
- **Glitter**
- Things with **Glitter** on them
- **Globes**
- **Gloves**
- **Glue**
- **Goggles** (ski, swimming, or work)
- **Gold**
- **Golf** stuff (clubs, balls, shoes, shirts, hats, bags, etc.)
- **Gowns** (wedding, prom, bridesmaid, etc.)
- **Green** items
- **Greeting** cards (ones you haven't given & probably never will, or ones you've received)
- **Grey** items
- **Gross** things
- Things on the **Ground**
- Things from a **Group** that you're no longer part of
- **Gum**
- **Guy** things

Find a few of these things that you no longer need, use, love, or have the space to store and let them go.

Write here the items you decluttered that begin with G:
_____
_____
_____
_____

"If a GIFT has come to you wrapped in obligations and tied tightly with a ribbon of guilt, then it's not really a gift at all. It's a manipulation. A gift should be something freely given that enhances your life and reminds you lovingly of the giver. If it's not, you simply should not give it a place in your home."
~ Peter Walsh

11. Decluttering "H" Things

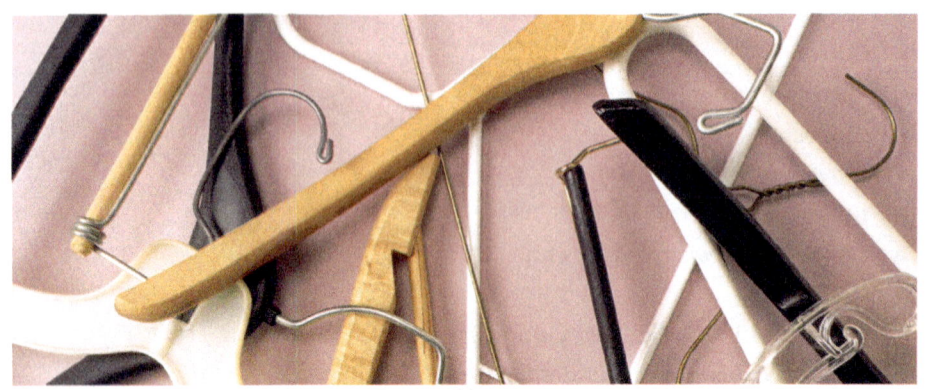

Image: Hangers

Ask for HELP if you get stuck

In this chapter you're decluttering items that begin with the letter H. You can declutter *anything you want* that begins with H. Choose any of the items below that resonate with you, or declutter your own ideas that begin with H.

Decluttering Ideas That Begin With The Letter H

Here are a few items or areas you may have in your home that you could declutter:
- **Hair** products
- **Half**-finished projects (that you know you'll never finish)
- **Hall** closet
- **Hallway**
- **Handkerchiefs**
- **Hand**-me-downs
- **Hand** products
- **Hangers**
- **Happy** meal toys
- **Hardcover** books
- **Hats**

- **Headbands**
- **Heating** blankets
- **Heat** packs
- Self-**Help** books
- **Hockey** equipment
- Things you have been **Holding** on to
- **Hoodies**
- Things on **Hooks**
- **Hoses**
- **Hotel** toiletries
- **Household** items
- Things you have **Hundreds** of

Find a few of these things that you no longer need, use, love, or have the space to store and let them go.

Write here the items you decluttered that begin with H:
_____
_____
_____
_____

"Until you are HAPPY with who you are, you will never be happy with what you have." ~ Zig Ziglar

12. Decluttering "I" Things

Image: Ice Packs

IMAGINE what your home will look like after decluttering

In this chapter you're decluttering items that begin with the letter I. You can declutter *anything you want* that begins with I. Choose any of the items below that resonate with you, or declutter your own ideas that begin with I.

Decluttering Ideas That Begin With The Letter I

Here are a few items or areas you may have in your home that you could declutter:

- **Icebox**
- **Ice** cream (freezer-burnt, back of the freezer stuff)
- **Ice** cream scoops
- **Ice** cube trays
- **Ice** packs
- **Ice** skates
- "**Icky**" stuff you've been holding onto that just needs to be thrown away
- **Ideas** (you know... all those "I want to do this someday" bits and pieces of things? or files with ideas you want to do)
- **In-progress** projects (that you know you won't finish)
- Old **Income** tax documents (check how long you need to keep them first)

- **Infant** clothing
- **Information** you were keeping in physical format that you can find online now
- **Inside** anything (a drawer, box, closet, etc.)
- **Instruction** manuals
- **Instruments**
- Things you're no longer **Interested** in (hobbies you've stopped doing, magazines you've stopped reading, etc.)
- **Investment** papers (for old investments or just old statements you don't need)
- **Invitations**

Find a few of these things that you no longer need, use, love, or have the space to store and let them go.

Write here the items you decluttered that begin with I:

_____
_____
_____
_____

"INSTEAD of thinking I am losing something when I clear clutter, I dwell on what I might gain." ~ Lisa J. Shultz

13. Decluttering "J" Things

Image: Jewelry

> **JUST jump in and get started**
> **(don't wait for the "perfect" time)**

In this chapter you're decluttering items that begin with the letter J. You can declutter *anything you want* that begins with J. Choose any of the items below that resonate with you, or declutter your own ideas that begin with J.

Decluttering Ideas That Begin With The Letter J

Here are a few items or areas you may have in your home that you could declutter:

- **Jackets**
- **Jacks**
- **Jam / Jelly**
- **Jammies**
- **Jars**
- **Jeans**
- **Jewelry**
- **Jewelry** boxes
- **Jigsaw** puzzles
- Stuff from previous **Jobs** that you no longer need
- **Jogging** pants/shoes

- **Journals**
- **Juggling** balls (actual or metaphorical ones)
- **Jugs**
- **Juice** pitchers
- **Jump** ropes
- **Junk** drawers
- **Junkmail**
- And of course there's always good ole' **Junk**!

Find a few of these things that you no longer need, use, love, or have the space to store and let them go.

Write here the items you decluttered that begin with J:

_____
_____
_____
_____

"JUST because something brought you joy in the past doesn't mean you need to keep it forever." ~ Joshua Becker

14. Decluttering "K" Things

Image: Keys

KEEP track of what you're letting go of to stay motivated

In this chapter you're decluttering items that begin with the letter K. You can declutter *anything you want* that begins with K. Choose any of the items below that resonate with you, or declutter your own ideas that begin with K.

Decluttering Ideas That Begin With The Letter K

Here are a few items or areas you may have in your home that you could declutter:
- Things you've been **Keeping** for no real reason
- **Keepsakes**
- **Keychains**
- **Keys**
- **Kickboxing** equipment
- **Kids'** bedrooms
- **Kids'** clothes
- **Kids'** toys
- Any **Kids'** stuff (but not your **Kids** - even though you may be tempted LOL!)
- **Kindergarten** items
- **Kitchen** appliances

- **Kitchen** cabinets
- **Kitchen** counters
- **Kitchen** drawers
- **Kitchen** gadgets
- **Kitchen** table
- Or your whole **Kitchen**
- **Kites**
- Craft **Kits**
- **Knee**-high socks
- **Knitting** supplies

Find a few of these things that you no longer need, use, love, or have the space to store and let them go.

Write here the items you decluttered that begin with K:
_____
_____
_____
_____

> *"KEEP only items that spark joy."* ~ Marie Kondo

15. Decluttering "L" Things

Image: Lego

LET go of the past so you can live in the present

In this chapter you're decluttering items that begin with the letter L. You can declutter *anything you want* that begins with L. Choose any of the items below that resonate with you, or declutter your own ideas that begin with L.

Decluttering Ideas That Begin With The Letter L

Here are a few items or areas you may have in your home that you could declutter:
- **Lace**
- **Ladders**
- **Lamps**
- **Lamp** shades
- **Laptops** (old ones that you don't use anymore)
- Things you have a **Large** number of
- Old **Laundry** detergent
- **Laundry** room
- Things that are **Laying** around
- **Leather** shoes (or boots or gloves or purses)
- **Leggings**

- **Lego**
- **Lemon** or **Lime** coloured things
- **Letters**
- **Lids** (that are missing containers/pots)
- **Lights**
- **Linen** closet
- **Linens**
- **Lipstick** (that is old or that you don't wear)
- **Liquor** (that is old or you won't finish - just drinking all day STILL doesn't count LOL!)
- **Lists**
- **Living** room
- **Lockets**
- **Locks**
- **Long**-overdue **Library** books (or anything **Long**-overdue!)
- **Long**-sleeved shirts
- Projects that are a **Lost** cause
- **Lounge** wear
- Things you don't **Love**
- **Lunch** containers

Find a few of these things that you no longer need, use, love, or have the space to store and let them go.

Write here the items you decluttered that begin with D:

_____
_____
_____
_____

"LOVE people, use things. The opposite never works." ~ The Minimalists

16. Decluttering "M" Things

Image: Markers

Listen to your favourite upbeat MUSIC

In this chapter you're decluttering items that begin with the letter M. You can declutter *anything you want* that begins with M. Choose any of the items below that resonate with you, or declutter your own ideas that begin with M.

Decluttering Ideas That Begin With The Letter M

Here are a few items or areas you may have in your home that you could declutter:
- Things that make you **Mad**
- Things you **Made** (or your kids **Made**)
- **Magazines**
- **Magnets**
- **Mail**
- **Main** bathroom
- **Main** bedroom
- **Main** closet
- **Make-up**
- **Make-up** bags
- **Maps**

DECLUTTERING FROM A TO Z

- **Marbles**
- Things you bought because they were **Marked** down
- **Markers**
- **Martini** glasses
- **Mascara**
- **Masks**
- **Mason** jars
- Things without a **Match/Mate**
- **Matchbox** cars
- **Mats**
- **Medical** supplies
- **Men's** stuff (e.g deodorant, body wash, etc. - make sure it's OK with him though!)
- **Messy** room
- **Messy** things
- **Microwave** (old ones still laying around)
- Anything that's not "**Mine**"
- Things that are **Mint** green
- **Mirrors**
- **Mitts/Mittens**
- **Monsters**
- **Mop** buckets
- **Mops**
- Old **Movie** tickets
- Things you have **Multiples** of (or too **Many** of)
- Expired **Multivitamins**
- **Music**

Find a few of these things that you no longer need, use, love, or have the space to store and let them go.

Write here the items you decluttered that begin with M:
_____
_____
_____
_____

45

> *"MINIMIZING our possessions blazes the way for life change. It frees up our life to pursue our greatest passions."* ~ Joshua Becker

DECLUTTERING FROM A TO Z

17. Decluttering "N" Things

Image: Nail Polish

It's NEVER too late to declutter

In this chapter you're decluttering items that begin with the letter N. You can declutter *anything you want* that begins with N. Choose any of the items below that resonate with you, or declutter your own ideas that begin with N.

Decluttering Ideas That Begin With The Letter N

Here are a few items or areas you may have in your home that you could declutter:

- **Nail** polish
- **Nails** (for construction or for your fingers)
- Things with your old **Name**
- **Napkins** (paper or linen)
- **Necklaces**
- **Neckties**
- **Needles** (knitting or otherwise)
- Things that bring back **Negative** memories
- Items that belong to your **Neighbours**
- **New** but probably **Never** going to wear clothes
- **New** items that need to be returned to the store

47

- **Newspapers**
- **Nightgowns**
- **Nightlights**
- **Night** table
- **Nose**-drops
- Things that are a **Nuisance**
- **Nursery**
- **Nuts** & bolts

Find a few of these things that you no longer need, use, love, or have the space to store and let them go.

Write here the items you decluttered that begin with N:

_____
_____
_____
_____

> *"Have NOTHING in your house that you do not know to be useful, or believe to be beautiful."* ~ William Morris

18. Decluttering "O" Things

Image: Ornaments

Recognize your OBSTACLES so you can OVERCOME them

In this chapter you're decluttering items that begin with the letter O. You can declutter *anything you want* that begins with O. Choose any of the items below that resonate with you, or declutter your own ideas that begin with O.

Decluttering Ideas That Begin With The Letter O

Here are a few items or areas you may have in your home that you could declutter:
- **Oak** furniture
- **Oars**
- **Occasionally** used items
- **Ocean** finds (shells, rocks, etc.)
- **Octopus/Owl/Ox** knick knacks or toys
- **Odds** and ends
- **Office** supplies
- **Official** documents (make sure it's no longer needed)
- **Oh**-I-don't-know-why-I-bought-this items
- **Oil** (kitchen, bath, garage)
- Rusty **Oil** cans

- **Oil** filters
- Essential **Oils**
- **Old** anything!
- **Old** books
- **Old** chairs
- **Old** clothes
- **Old** windows
- **Olive** (green) items
- Sets with only **One** left
- **Open** packets of stuff you will probably never finish
- Items that are **Opposite** to what you're trying to achieve
- **Optical** supplies
- Things that are **Orange**
- **Organizing** products you don't need
- **Ornaments**
- **Orthodontic** supplies (leftover elastics, wax strips, etc.)
- **Orthotics**
- **Ottomans** (the actual ottoman or the stuff inside)
- Things that help with **Ouch** (first aid kits, meds, heating pads, hot water bottles, etc.)
- **Outdoor** furniture
- **Outgrown** clothes
- **Out**-of-date items
- **Out**-of-season clothes
- **Outside** toys
- **Oval** shaped items
- **Oven** cleaning supplies or equipment
- **Overalls**
- **Overflow** items (pantry, toiletries, supplies, etc.)

Find a few of these things that you no longer need, use, love, or have the space to store and let them go.

Write here the items you decluttered that begin with O:
_____
_____
_____
_____

"OUTER order contributes to inner calm." ~ Gretchen Rubin

19. Decluttering "P" Things

Image: Paint Brushes

PRETEND you're moving-would you pack and unpack this item?

In this chapter you're decluttering items that begin with the letter P. You can declutter *anything you want* that begins with P. Choose any of the items below that resonate with you, or declutter your own ideas that begin with P.

Decluttering Ideas That Begin With The Letter P

Here are a few items or areas you may have in your home that you could declutter:

- **Paint**
- **Paint** brushes
- **Paintings**
- **Pencils**
- **Pens**
- **People** (toxic ones you don't want in your life!)
- **Perfume**
- **Pet** supplies
- Apps on your **Phone**
- **Phones**
- **Pictures/Photos**

- Games that are missing **Pieces**
- **Postcards**
- **Pots** and **Pans**
- Expired/unnecessary **Prescriptions**
- **Pretty** messy areas
- **Products** you no longer use
- **Protein Powder**
- **Purses**
- **Puzzles**

Find a few of these things that you no longer need, use, love, or have the space to store and let them go.

Write here the items you decluttered that begin with P:

_____
_____
_____
_____

"PICTURE your dream home. I bet it's not filled with clutter." ~ Joshua Becker

20. Decluttering "Q" Things

Image: Quilts

Make QUICK decisions and don't second guess yourself

In this chapter you're decluttering items that begin with the letter Q. You can declutter *anything you want* that begins with Q. Choose any of the items below that resonate with you, or declutter your own ideas that begin with Q.

Decluttering Ideas That Begin With The Letter Q

Here are a few items or areas you may have in your home that you could declutter:

- **Qtips**
- Things that **Quack**
- Items you have **Quadruple** of
- Poor **Quality** items
- Stuff you have a large **Quantity** of
- **Quart** jars
- **Quartz**
- Things you only use if a **Queen** was coming to visit
- **Queen**-sized bed or sheets or pillows
- Things you **Question** why you bought
- Things that are not **Quiet**

DECLUTTERING FROM A TO Z

- **Quilting** stuff (scraps of fabric just in case!)
- **Quilts**
- **Quirky** items
- Items from hobbies/activities that you've **Quit**
- Clothes that are **Quite** large/small
- Your kids' **Quizzes** (or other schoolwork)

Find a few of these things that you no longer need, use, love, or have the space to store and let them go.

Write here the items you decluttered that begin with Q:

_____
_____
_____
_____

> *"The QUESTION of what you want to own is also the question of how you want to live your life."* ~ Marie Kondo

21. Decluttering "R" Things

Image: Receipts

> **RECOGNIZE what you're buying so you can avoid future clutter**

In this chapter you're decluttering items that begin with the letter R. You can declutter *anything you want* that begins with R. Choose any of the items below that resonate with you, or declutter your own ideas that begin with R.

Decluttering Ideas That Begin With The Letter R

Here are a few items or areas you may have in your home that you could declutter:

- **Rackets**
- **Radios**
- **Rags**
- **Rain** gear (coats, boots, umbrellas, etc.)
- **Rakes**
- Things you bought when you weren't **Rational**
- Things you **Realistically** will never use
- **Really** old things
- **Really** ugly things
- Stuff you have for no **Reason**
- **Receipts**

- Gifts you **Received** but don't like/use
- **Recipes** (from magazines/books that you haven't made and probably won't)
- Things that fill you with **Regret**
- Items from **Relatives**
- **Remotes**
- Things you planned to **Repurpose** but never did
- Things you need to **Return**
- Anything you can get **Rid** of to **Reduce** the clutter in your home
- **Rooms** you haven't decluttered yet
- **Ruined** clothes (that are **Ripped** or beyond **Repair**)
- **Rum** (you know the drill here LOL!)
- **Rusty** items

Find a few of these things that you no longer need, use, love, or have the space to store and let them go.

Write here the items you decluttered that begin with R:
_____
_____
_____
_____

"REMEMBER: you are not what you own. Storing all those books doesn't make you any smarter; it just makes your life more cluttered." ~ Francine Jay

22. Decluttering "S" Things

Image: Stuffed Animals

SIMPLIFY your life by having less

In this chapter you're decluttering items that begin with the letter S. You can declutter *anything you want* that begins with S. Choose any of the items below that resonate with you, or declutter your own ideas that begin with S.

Decluttering Ideas That Begin With The Letter S

Here are a few items or areas you may have in your home that you could declutter:
- **Safety** items (when your kids have outgrown the childproofing things)
- **Salad** bowls/tongs/dressings
- Things you bought on **Sale** but don't really need
- Cans of **Salmon** or **Soup**
- **Sandals**
- **Sandbox** toys
- **Sandpaper**
- **Saucers**
- **Scarves**
- Things you don't like the **Scent** of
- **School Supplies**

- **School** work (your old stuff or your kids')
- **Screens**
- **Screwdrivers** (the tools not the drink LOL)
- **Scrubbies**
- Items that have been clutter for so long you don't even **See** them anymore
- **Shampoo**
- **Shaving** lotion
- **Sheets**
- **Shells**
- **Shelves**
- **Shirts**
- **Shoulder** pads
- Things in your **Shower**
- **Shower** caddy
- **Shower** gel
- **Side** table
- Things you bought when you were **Sightseeing**
- **Silver** earrings/necklaces/etc.
- **Silverware**
- Items that are **Similar** to each other
- Things you've had since you were **Single**
- **Skis** (or **Ski** equipment)
- **Sleds**
- **Slow** cooker
- **Smoke** detectors
- **Soap** (little pieces left over or whole bars you won't use)
- **Socks**
- **Softcover** books
- **Software**
- **Something** (just find **Something**!)
- **Songs** (from your phone/ipod)
- **Spices**
- **Sponges**
- **Spray** paint
- **Sprays** you don't use (cleaners, air fresheners, etc.)
- **Spring/Summer** clothes

- **Spring** jackets
- **Stacks** of papers/magazines/books
- Things on your **Steps**
- **Stereos**
- **Storage** bins
- **Storage** room
- Anything that makes you **Stressed**
- **Stuffed** toys
- Any kind of **Supplies**
- Flat **Surfaces**
- **Sweaters**
- **Sweatshirts**
- **Swimsuits**
- And my personal favourite... **Stuff** (or maybe you like that other **S** word instead)

Find a few of these things that you no longer need, use, love, or have the space to store and let them go.

Write here the items you decluttered that begin with S:
_____
_____
_____
_____

> "A SIMPLIFIED life means that what has to get done will get done. And when we pare down life to its simplest, most beautifully basic parts, we're left with room to enjoy each other, to rest, and to truly savor life with all our hearts, minds, and spirits." ~ Emily Ley

23. Decluttering "T" Things

Image: Tools

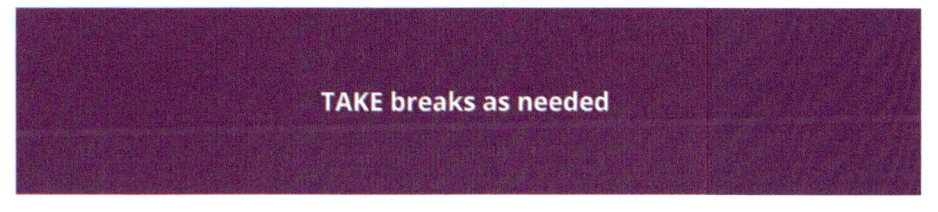

TAKE breaks as needed

In this chapter you're decluttering items that begin with the letter T. You can declutter *anything you want* that begins with T. Choose any of the items below that resonate with you, or declutter your own ideas that begin with T.

Decluttering Ideas That Begin With The Letter T

Here are a few items or areas you may have in your home that you could declutter:
- **Table** (the stuff on it or an actual extra table)
- **Table Tennis** items
- **Take-out** containers
- **Tank** tops
- Very old **Tax** documents
- **Tea**
- **Tea** cups
- **Technology**
- Stuff from when you were a **Teenager**
- **Telephone** numbers
- **Telephones**

- **Televisions**
- **Tennis** racquets/balls
- **Tents**
- **Thermometers**
- Things you bought on a **Trip**
- Things you have **Tons** of
- **Thread**
- **Threadbare** socks/clothes
- **Ties**
- **Tires**
- **To**-do list
- **Tools**
- Items that are **Torn**
- Items you haven't **Touched** in years
- **Toys**
- **Trays**
- **Treadmills**
- **Trinkets**
- **Truck**
- **Tshirts**
- Items you have **Two** or **Three** of
- And if you'd like a nice general all-encompassing category for today... just go with **Things**!

Find a few of these things that you no longer need, use, love, or have the space to store and let them go.

Write here the items you decluttered that begin with T:
_____
_____
_____
_____

> *"THE more you have, the more you are occupied. The less you have, the more free you are."* ~ Mother Teresa

24. Decluttering "U" Things

Image: Utensils

Be honest about what you actually USE

In this chapter you're decluttering items that begin with the letter U. You can declutter *anything you want* that begins with U. Choose any of the items below that resonate with you, or declutter your own ideas that begin with U.

Decluttering Ideas That Begin With The Letter U

Here are a few items or areas you may have in your home that you could declutter:
- **Ugly** old clothes
- **Umbrella** hats
- **Umbrellas**
- **Under** the bed
- Things you don't **Understand** why you bought them
- **Underwear/Unmentionables**
- **Undesirable** items
- Stuff that makes you feel **Uneasy**
- Things that seem **Unending**
- People or emails to **Unfollow/Unsubscribe**
- Items that make you **Unhappy**

63

- **Unidentified** objects
- **Uniforms**
- Things in storage **Units**
- Stuff that goes **Unnoticed**
- Items that were **Unplanned** (kids don't count LOL!)
- **Unused** items
- **Unwanted** things
- Items that have been **Updated**
- Things that cause an **Uproar**
- **Utensils** (everyday, fancy, serving/cooking, BBQ)
- **Utility** room/drawer

Find a few of these things that you no longer need, use, love, or have the space to store and let them go.

Write here the items you decluttered that begin with U:

_____
_____
_____
_____

"UNDER the influence of clutter, we may underestimate how much time we're giving to the less important stuff." ~ Zoë Kim

25. Decluttering "V" Things

Image: VHS Tapes

> How much you VALUE an item isn't necessarily how much it's worth

In this chapter you're decluttering items that begin with the letter V. You can declutter *anything you want* that begins with V. Choose any of the items below that resonate with you, or declutter your own ideas that begin with V.

Decluttering Ideas That Begin With The Letter V

Here are a few items or areas you may have in your home that you could declutter:

- Things that you got on **Vacation**
- **Vacation** photos
- **Vacuum** cleaners (or old parts)
- **Van**
- Old/extra **Vanilla** products
- Stuff that keeps **Vanishing**
- Good ole' "**Various**" items
- **Varnish**
- Stuff you have a **Vast** quantity of
- **VCR's**
- **Vehicle**

- Items that you haven't used in a **Very** long time
- **Vests**
- **VHS** tapes
- **Vicious** hangers (you know... the wire ones that get all tangled together!)
- Something that will make you feel **Victorious**
- **Videos**
- **Vinaigrette** dressings
- Things made of **Vinyl**
- Things that are **Violet**
- Items that are **Visually** distracting
- Old **Vitamins**
- **V-necks**

Find a few of these things that you no longer need, use, love, or have the space to store and let them go.

Write here the items you decluttered that begin with V:

_____
_____
_____
_____

"If that 'VALUABLE' figurine you inherited from your grandmother is selling for $9.99 on eBay, then it's time to wake up and smell the coffee." ~ Peter Walsh

26. Decluttering "W" Things

Image: Wood

Ask yourself "WHAT if I didn't have this?" Let it go if you can borrow it or if you have something else you can use instead

In this chapter you're decluttering items that begin with the letter W. You can declutter *anything you want* that begins with W. Choose any of the items below that resonate with you, or declutter your own ideas that begin with W.

Decluttering Ideas That Begin With The Letter W

Here are a few items or areas you may have in your home that you could declutter:

- Things you see when you **Walk** around your home
- Items hanging on your **Wall**
- **Wallets**
- **Wallpaper**
- **Wands**
- **Warranties**
- **Washcloths**
- **Waste**
- Things that **Waste** time
- **Wastebaskets**
- **Watches**

- **Water** bottles
- Stuff that was damaged by **Water**
- **Watersport** equipment
- **Wax**
- Clothes you don't **Wear** any more
- **Wedding** dress
- **Wedding** memorabilia
- **Weights**
- **Well**-intentioned ideas that never really materialized
- **Wet Wipes** that are no longer **Wet**
- **Wheelbarrow**
- Things that make you **Wheezy**
- **Whisks**
- **Whistles**
- **Whiteboards**
- **White** things
- Items made of **Wicker**
- **Wigs**
- **Wii** consoles/games/accessories/controllers
- **Windows**
- **Winter** gear
- **Wires**
- Items that are no longer **Wonderful**
- Things you know you **Won't** use
- **Wood**
- Things made of **Wood**
- **Wool**
- **Wool** sweaters
- **Word** files on your computer
- Stuff from **Work** that you don't need anymore
- Things that don't **Work**
- **Workshop**
- Items that are **Worn** out
- **Wrap**

Find a few of these things that you no longer need, use, love, or have the space to store and let them go.

Write here the items you decluttered that begin with W:

_____
_____
_____
_____

"WANTING less is a better blessing than having more." ~ Mary Ellen Edmunds

27. Decluttering "X" Things

Image: Xbox Controller and Games

X marks the spot for treasure! Keep the things you really love and let go of those that are not treasures

In this chapter you're decluttering items that begin with the letter X. You can declutter *anything you want* that begins with X. Choose any of the items below that resonate with you, or declutter your own ideas that begin with X.

Decluttering Ideas That Begin With The Letter X

Here are a few items or areas you may have in your home that you could declutter:
- Stuff that belongs to your **eX**
- Things that aren't **eXcellent**
- **EXcess** things
- Areas near **eXits**
- **EXpectations** that are too high
- **UneXplained** items
- Anything with a Roman numeral **X** in/on it
- **Xbox** consoles/games/accessories/controllers
- **Xerox** machines/copies
- **Xmas** Decorations
- **X-rated** clothes/lingerie

- **X-rays**
- **Xtra** large piece of glass (or anything **Xtra** large)
- **Xtras** you don't or won't use
- **Xtreme** sports gear
- **Xylophones**

Find a few of these things that you no longer need, use, love, or have the space to store and let them go.

Write here the items you decluttered that begin with X:
_____
_____
_____
_____

> *"Fill your life with EXPERIENCES, not things. Have stories to tell, not stuff to show."* ~ Unknown

28. Decluttering "Y" Things

Image: Yarn

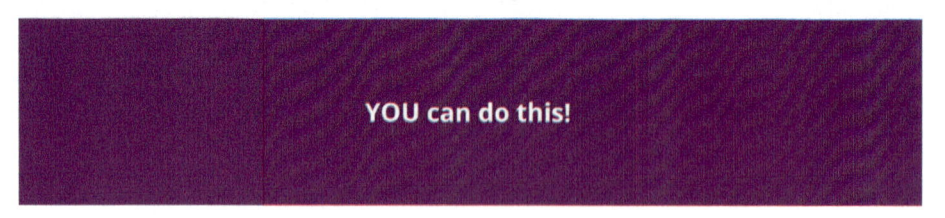

YOU can do this!

In this chapter you're decluttering items that begin with the letter Y. You can declutter *anything you want* that begins with Y. Choose any of the items below that resonate with you, or declutter your own ideas that begin with Y.

Decluttering Ideas That Begin With The Letter Y

Here are a few items or areas you may have in your home that you could declutter:

- **Yard** furniture
- Random junk in your **Yard**
- Things you bought at a **Yard** sale
- **Yardsticks**
- **Yard** toys
- **Yarn**
- Things that make you **Yawn**
- Items you haven't used in over a **Year**
- Things you only use once a **Year**
- Stuff from **Years** gone by
- Things that make you **Yell**

- Items that are **Yellow**
- Things you shouldn't have said **Yes** to
- **Yoga** mats, blocks, bands
- Expired **Yogurt**
- Items from when you were **Young**(er)
- Things from your **Youngest** child's room
- Anything that is **Yours**
- **Yucky** stuff

Find a few of these things that you no longer need, use, love, or have the space to store and let them go.

Write here the items you decluttered that begin with Y:

_____
_____
_____
_____

> *"YOU say, 'If I had a little more, I should be very satisfied.' You make a mistake. If you are not content with what you have, you would not be satisfied if it were doubled."* ~ Charles Spurgeon

29. Decluttering "Z" Things

Caption: Zoo Animals

Make sure you're getting lots of ZZZ's so you can make good decisions

In this chapter you're decluttering items that begin with the letter Z. You can declutter *anything you want* that begins with Z. Choose any of the items below that resonate with you, or declutter your own ideas that begin with Z.

Decluttering Ideas That Begin With The Letter Z

Here are a few items or areas you may have in your home that you could declutter:

- **Zebra** print clothes/accessories
- **Zebra** statues
- Items that don't make your home feel **Zen**-like
- Things made of **Zephyr**
- Stuff that brings you **Zero** joy
- Things you have a **Zillion** of
- **Zinc** cream
- **Zippers**
- Things you bought at a **Zoo**
- **Zoo** animal toys
- **Zoo** stickers

- **Zoom** lenses
- **Zumba** DVD's

Find a few of these things that you no longer need, use, love, or have the space to store and let them go.

Write here the items you decluttered that begin with Z:
_____
_____
_____
_____
_____

> *"When one's expectations are reduced to ZERO, one really appreciates everything one does have."* ~ Stephen Hawking

30. What Now?

You did it! You decluttered from A to Z. Way to go! Take a moment and think about all you've accomplished.

How Did You Do Decluttering From A To Z?

How many items did you declutter while you went through this book?
_____
_____
_____

How does your home feel as a result of all your hard work? What are you most excited about in your less-cluttered home?
_____
_____
_____

Look back to chapter one where you wrote out your motivation for decluttering. Is it still your motivation today? If not, what is your motivation now?
_____
_____
_____

Did you achieve the decluttering goals you set in chapter 2? How do you feel about your decluttering efforts? Can you see progress after your hard work this month?
_____
_____
_____

I hope you can see a huge difference after decluttering through the alphabet! Obviously, if your clutter has built up over many years, it's not going to disappear in a short amount of time. But hopefully some of these things are true for you:

- You're more relaxed in your home
- You can find things when you look for them
- You're able to have people over without being embarrassed by the clutter
- You can eat at your dining table again
- You're more productive

Whatever your motivation is, continue to keep it in mind so you can keep your home clutter-free. You could even create a little poster or sign with your motivation on it and hang it somewhere you will see it regularly and be reminded of it. Perhaps include some pictures of your clutter-free spaces that you worked so hard on, to remind you how it feels to have less clutter in your home.

Reward Yourself!

You've worked hard and you deserve a treat! That may be a nap or a long relaxing bubble bath. Maybe you reward yourself with a mani-pedi with a friend who will celebrate with you. If you decluttered a lot of clothing this month, maybe you treat yourself to one (and I mean one!) new shirt (although I don't recommend this if shopping is a typical way you reward yourself... it's better to replace that habit with something that won't result in future clutter).

You know what will be the best reward for you. Choose something and celebrate all your hard work.

How will you reward yourself?

_____
_____
_____

Develop New Habits

Now is the time to establish a few new habits to help keep the clutter from coming back. Here are a few that may be helpful:

- **Follow the "one in, one out" rule**. Or if you still have a lot of clutter, maybe "one in, three out" would be better. So, if you buy a new sweater, give away one you don't wear. If you buy a new kitchen gadget, donate one you don't use as much. It sounds simple, but you have to be very diligent with this to maintain the level of "stuff" you have in your home.
- **Put things away every single day**. Surfaces are clutter magnets and it is so easy for them to become covered by just leaving a few items to put away later. This clutter is quickly multiplied if there are multiple people doing this. Stop clutter in its tracks by putting things away when you are finished with them!
- **Entertain on a regular basis**. The best way to keep your home uncluttered is to have people over. It will motivate you to tidy your home. If you need to do this every week then do that. Or every 2 weeks. Whatever works best for you. And don't just hide everything in a closet before your guests arrive. That's not decluttering and you'll end up back where you were!
- **Start giving clutter-free gifts** to the people who live in your home (or anyone really!). Consider giving consumable gifts or experiences. These won't result in more clutter entering your home. You can't control what other people give your family members, but at least you can reduce your clutter impact.

If you work on these habits, you'll continue to enjoy your clutter-free home for years to come!

Write out which new habits you'll start doing to help keep your home clutter-free:

_____
_____

Ways to Continue Your Decluttering Journey

If you still have clutter in your home, **keep decluttering**! You're all warmed up now, so it should be even easier to let go of things.

1. **Go through the Decluttering From A To Z book all over again**! We've done the challenge this book was inspired by in the 365 Items in 365 Days group many times and every time people found new things to declutter. You'll find the same, I'm sure!

2. **Join the 365 Items in 365 Days Facebook group!** It really is an encouraging and supportive place, full of other declutterers, just like you!

3. **Check out my 31 Days of Easy Decluttering series on my blog**. Each post gives tips to declutter different items or areas of your home. If you're focusing on certain areas of your home some of the posts may help you out.

4. **Sign up for my newsletter to get monthly tips right in your inbox.** Use this link: http://eepurl.com/it1oss or the QR code below.

How are you going to continue on your decluttering journey?

_____
_____
_____

Share Your Decluttering Progress!

I hope all the ideas from this book helped you declutter your home! Make sure you share your progress with the people you told in chapter 1. And if you share online, use the hashtag #DeclutteringFromAtoZ so I can see your progress!

Happy decluttering!

RESOURCES

Check out my decluttering group, blog series, and the printable decluttering signs I mentioned:
- The 365 Items in 365 Days Facebook group
  https://www.facebook.com/groups/365ItemsIn365Days
- The 31 Days of Easy Decluttering series on my blog
  https://fromoverwhelmedtoorganized.com/31-days-of-easy-decluttering/
- Printable Decluttering Signs
  https://fromoverwhelmedtoorganized.com/printable-signs-to-help-you-declutter/

Read more from some of the organizing professionals I quoted and their perspectives on decluttering here:

Joshua Becker: https://www.becomingminimalist.com/books/
Francine Jay: https://www.missminimalist.com/books/
Zoë Kim: https://raisingsimple.com/book-minimalism-for-families/
Marie Kondo: https://shop.konmari.com/collections/books
Emily Ley: https://emilyleybooks.com/library
Kathy Lipp: https://www.kathilipp.com/books/
The Minimalists: https://www.theminimalists.com/books/
Tsh Oxenreider: https://www.tshoxenreider.com/books
Gretchen Rubin: https://gretchenrubin.com/books/
Lisa J. Shultz: https://lisajshultz.com/books/
Peter Walsh: https://peterwalshdesign.com/books-video

I hope these resources help you go from overwhelmed to organized!

BONUS!

As a bonus for purchasing this book, I'm offering you a complimentary 30-minute virtual consultation.

You can ask me any decluttering or organizing questions, and I can give you personalized tips for your home.

Simply forward your receipt and let me know you'd like to book your bonus: Hilda@FromOverwhelmedToOrganized

FREE!

ABOUT THE AUTHOR

Hilda Rodgers is a Professional Organizer who founded From Overwhelmed To Organized in 2013, after starting a blog by the same name in 2012. She loves helping overwhelmed people declutter and organize their homes so they can spend more time with the people they love, doing the things they are passionate about.

In 2014, Hilda started a Facebook group called 365 Items in 365 Days where she encourages people from around the world to declutter, one item at a time.

Hilda is a Gold Leaf member of the Professional Organizers in Canada and is a Trained Professional Organizer. She is the Chair of their national education committee and Past Chair of her local chapter. She is also a subscriber of the Institute for Challenging Disorganization ("ICD") and has earned her Level 1 Foundation Certificate of Study in Chronic Disorganization, Level 1 Certificate of Study in ADHD, and is continuing to work towards other certificates through ICD.

Over the last several years, Hilda has won numerous awards including the prestigious Professional Organizers in Canada Harold Taylor award, Readers' Choice Mississauga awards, Community Votes Mississauga awards and Canadian Choice Awards.

Hilda is a speaker, both online and in person, sharing decluttering and organizing tips for various audiences, including GE Canada, Kitty Talk TV Show, and the Women's Entrepreneur Conference. She also enjoys making a difference in her local community through supporting various charities.

Together with her husband and two teenagers, Hilda lives in Mississauga, Ontario, Canada. She loves anything purple and everything chocolate.

Printed in Great Britain
by Amazon